The Infinite Souls

21 Poems about Love and Hope

Tarana Singhal

India | USA | UK

Dedication

I dedicate this book to my family, friends, and everyone who believed in me, I am indebted to you all.

Preface

This book is a compilation of moments of adoration, crushes, infatuations, hope, and self-love. With this, I celebrate all the love in the world, for god, ourselves, and the beautiful people we meet.

Acknowledgements

Big cheers to my wonderful mom and dad who raised me to be a strong, independent girl, unafraid to go after what I dream of, always supporting me through the thick and thin of life.

1. Divine Love

How I feel
I cannot express
The love I have
The love I am
It is not like an ocean
For it has no bottom
It is like the sky
Limitless and infinite
It makes me strong
It makes me centered
I feel true happiness
I feel true gratitude
It cannot be claimed
It has no name
For it cannot be expressed
Using twenty-six characters
There is renunciation
There is reverence
This love is impersonal
It just exists

It is divine love
The love for my god
That is in my soul
It is not an emotion
It is my very existence

2. What Love Is

What love is I wonder
Is it staring at the moon
And longing to be with you
Or is it feeling water waves in the ocean
Is it a cool breeze on a sunny day
My love, I don't know
But to me, it is looking at you smile
The way your eyes sparkle
When you talk about your favorite things
It is how you blush
When I catch you looking at me
It is how I adore you
How your fingers come together when you think
It is the moan that escapes your lips
When we kiss
What love is I don't know
But to me it's you
You are my definition of love

3. Dreams

I won't stop dreaming
Of all the things
That fills me with hope
Like rainbows and unicorns
Like hearts and flowers
Like angels and their bow
Like love and eternal vows
Like stars and faraway galaxies
Like fairies and their magic
I'm made that way
And I like being so

4. I Love How

I love how the sun
Smiles with the clouds

I love how the sky
Dances with the wind

I love how the ocean
Feels the sand

I love how the river
Shapes the rocks

I love how the moon
Talks to the stars

I love how the darkness
Loves the light

I love how the rainbow
Creates magic

5. At The Crack Of Dawn

Four in the morning
And the sky is dark
Birds chirping outside
It seems, happy they are
I couldn't sleep tonight
Thinking about my past
Nothing the bad things
Just the pleasant parts
I stand on the balcony
As I watch the sunrise
I listen to my memories
Stories that tell me
How far I've come
From the start
Realization dawns
As I reason my thoughts
There are things I want to do
The desires of my heart
There seems no better day
Except for this one to start

Night has come to an end
And so has the dark
Sunshine brings me another day
In this journey called life
To live by the heart

6. Fifteen Things I Hate About You

I hate how I keep looking at my phone
Waiting for your text as I keep missing you

I hate how my cheeks hurt from smiling
When they never had before

I hate how the kindness of your heart and the funny
dumb things you say
Make me feel butterflies in my stomach

I hate how I want to hear your voice
Feel your heartbeat and make you mine

I hate how I want you to tell me I am the most beautiful
girl
You have ever laid eyes on and ask me to be yours

I hate how completely unaware you are
Of the charming and handsome man that I see you as

I hate how much I love your perfectly imperfect self
Which I'm not sure I deserve to have

I hate how like and alike we are and yet
It feels like an imperfectly perfect match

I hate how I doubt myself and do not believe
How non-judgemental you are

I hate how much I love you for making me do things
I want to be the best version of myself

I hate how you always end up saying all the right things
and
That makes me wonder what kind of mind-reading skills
you have

I hate how much I fear losing you when
We have only just had the chance to have met

I hate how you are breaking the walls around my heart
And making me feel things I did not know I can

I hate how much I want you to kiss me, hold me and
Tell me all the things that make you the person that you
are

But most of all I hate how I can not tell you how hard
You have made me fall for you as I do not know if you
have fallen for me too

7. In Love With Myself

The feeling in my chest
How much I love myself
It keeps me moving forward
Leaving behind the mess
I am so grateful for what I have
Happiness and love
It makes me shine brighter
Then I ever have before
I am floating in the air
Dancing in my rain
My soul is on fire
Nothing disturbs me anymore
I have made peace with myself
Got control over my emotions
I am better than my best
I am in love with me so much
No one could ever mess with that
It is a beautiful feeling
Some say I am self-obsessed
But it doesn't matter

As long as I am smiling
Looking in the mirror
Content with who I am

8. Our Story Will Be A Legend

I was a fool
When I thought I had loved before
I was a fool
To think I knew what love was
I was a fool
To think it was just one feeling

Since I met you
My emotions have been overridden
Since I met you
I have laughed too much and cried
Since I met you
I have experienced emotions all new

I really thought
We could be just friends
I really thought
You would care as much as I do
I really thought

This could go on forever

Now it seems
Our meeting was fate's cruel joke
Now it seems
The concept of us was just one sided
Now it seems
My love is being tested by forces unknown

It's high time
Just be truthful of what you feel
It's high time
Just stay forever or permanently leave
It's high time
To establish foundations for the future if there is

In my heart
I will love you forever
In my heart
Our story will be a legend
In my heart
We will always be together

As for you
You can have me or lose me
As for you
I hope you choose to stay

As for you
It is now or never

9. Grateful

The feeling in my chest
How much I love myself
It keeps me moving forward
Leaving behind the mess

I am so grateful for what I have
Love and happiness
It is a beautiful feeling
I am better than my best

The feeling in my chest
It's like floating in the air
Or dancing in the rain
My soul is on fire

No regrets from the past
No fear of the future
Just being who I am
At peace with myself

10. Miss You

The air around
Misses your fragrance
The empty hallways
Call your name
A day without you
Seems so unbearable
I'm not at all alone
But this loneliness
Seems to creep around
Yearning to see you
Those innocent touches
Feel your presence
See your sweet smile
Look into your eyes
Your exasperated sigh
And silent laughter
You setting your hair with
Head tilted up and closed eyes
Flirting with you as
You look down with a shy smile

And that cute look
As I keep talking about
Anything that comes to my mind
Your time-traveling ability
As you stare into nothing
Then bringing you back here
I like how you show care
I even miss your irritating side
Like when you do things
You know will annoy me
The words don't stop flowing
But all I'm saying is
I miss all of you
With everything in me
So please stay close honey

11. Broken Star

You've been to me
What the moon is to stars
Always looking up to you
I've healed my darkest scars

Nights spent in your arms
Are full of love & moonlight
You give me a sort of calm
I never before could find

Meeting you in this lifetime
Seems universe's reward to me
For all the good deeds I ever did
My every wish that got accepted

Maybe sometimes there are clouds
That seems so threatening
But I can feel you always still
Enlightening my night sky

I was just a broken star
It was you who made me whole
It is with you that I shine
Brighter than I ever knew I could

12. Roses

I look at them
The roses in my hand
Old and withered
The time has fled
But their fragrance still
Enlightens my soul
Our love with time
Has only grown
The roses look just as beautiful
As the day you gave them
The beautiful roses
A symbol of our love
A love so pure
A love only ours

13. Get Up And Smile

When your heart cries
And your mind flies
You tell yourself
You will be alright

So, get up and smile
Don't you dare hide
It's time to shine
Power up and smile

Storms to weather
Mountains to climb
There is no time
To look behind

14. We Will Meet Again Darling

We'll meet again darling
When the sun shines
And the moon smiles

With glee the lake cries
And the north star sings
Some lovely lullabies

We'll meet again my love
When the day wanes
Into night skies

And the rain dances
To the intervening light
Of our souls alight

We'll meet again, I promise
When the time is right
And the wind blows by our side

That day we'll be most alive
Like the very first day
When your eyes met mine

15. Fire In The Rain

She stays quiet about things
It's just a quest for inner peace
Don't test her patience too much
Or the fierce fire inside her
Will burn you, skin you alive
She's building empires by herself
And needs no one by her side
Your presence will be valued
Your absence won't matter at all
So don't you dare think otherwise
She has always been an angel
Don't wake up her demonic side
She's the burning fire in the rain
She's the music that makes blood sing
She's everything she'll ever need

16. I Want To

I want to be the moon
In your dark sky

I want to be the color
That fills up your life

I want to be the words
Telling the story of your life

I want to be the melody
Of your favorite song

I want to be the lips
You kiss so passionately

I want to be your favorite drink
You sip so deviously

I want to be the only soul
Making your heart race

I want to be the dreams
You see in your sleep

17. Note To Self

A note to self
Take a little rest
Don't you worry girl
It's all for the best

Time is flowing
Bathe in its scent
The sun goes down
So, the moon can shine

The thing about life
Happiness is its quest
Requirements, just yourself
No need for anybody else

Curve balls come
You just got to bat
It's all about elegance
Through all of life's tests

It will all sum up
Don't create unrest
Chaos is gorgeous
Free your inner self

When it feels like war
Your kindness is the crown
Inner strength, the shield
And courage is your sword

So, don't you ever stop
Believe in yourself
Create your own destiny
Leave fate in god's hands

18. You Are My

You are my beautiful dream
You are the melody of my music
You are the words that fill up my poems
You are the color in my paintings
You are the music in my world
You are my infinite universe
You are the smile on my face
You are the love that lights my heart
You are the eternity my soul longs for
You are my happy place
You are my peace in silence
You are my song of the rain

19. Two Souls

Two souls, when they met
Exploded! Oh, such a mess
They were yellow and red
With time, from the ashes
Like a phoenix, they rose
All orange and fiery
Like the flames of hell
But the blinding beauty
Of their souls entwined
A magic not known
To the mortal world
So, to heaven, they fled
Towards the white light
Where peace resides
And blessings manifest
A godly kingdom ruled by love
Where bide the wise and kind

20. I Love You Like

I love you like the stars love the moon
Your love luminous in my dark sky

I love you like the ocean loves the sand
Kissing you with every rising wave

I love you like the sun loves the night
Missing you with every breath I take

I love you like the mountains love the sky
Feeling you close however far you may seem

I love you like the desert loves the lake
My thirsty soul longing for your soothing touch

I love you like I could never even begin to explain
A love with no end where all reasonings fail

21. Moon's Daughter And Sun's Warrior

I am the daughter of the moon
And every night I weep in her arms
She heals me from my dark side
Letting me sleep off my anxiety and hide
Giving me solitude a home to just be
The thing I thought I needed so desperately
She lets me forget my past, my burdens
Just for a little while longer, I stay
Until one night, she bids me goodbye
Reminds me of that day I needed to face
"It's time, my dear," she says

That morning, I faced the sun
Looked him right in the eye
"Hello, my warrior!" He chimed
Welcoming me with an iron embrace
Fatherly strength on bright display
He reminded me of my fighting days
Of times when I conquered my greatest fears

Burning my sins, taking away my guilt
He let me rise and end my sleepless nights
I ward off the evil controlling my mind
Finally letting go, as I get ready to battle

www.ingramcontent.com/pod-product-compliance
Lightning Source LLC
LaVergne TN
LVHW041246200726
843507LV00013B/2830